Black Fens Viral

Also by Frances Presley

The Sex of Art (2nd edition *)
Hula-Hoop
Linocut
Neither the One nor the Other, *with Elizabeth James*
Automatic Cross Stitch, *with Irma Irsara*
Somerset Letters
Paravane
Myne *
Lines of Sight *
Stone settings, *with Tilla Brading*
An Alphabet for Alina, *with Peterjon Skelt*
Halse for Hazel *
Sallow
Ada Unseen *
ADADADA, *with Tilla Brading*
Collected Poems Vol. 1 *
Collected Poems Vol. 2 *

** Shearsman publications*

Black Fens Viral

Frances Presley

Shearsman Books

First published in the United Kingdom in 2025 by
Shearsman Books Ltd
PO Box 4239
Swindon
SN3 9FN

Shearsman Books Ltd Registered Office
30–31 St. James Place, Mangotsfield, Bristol BS16 9JB
(this address not for correspondence)

EU AUTHORISED REPRESENTATIVE:
Lightning Source France
1 Av. Johannes Gutenberg, 78310 Maurepas, France
Email: compliance@lightningsource.fr

www.shearsman.com

ISBN 978-1-84861-988-3

CONTENTS

Images

All images from *An Introduction to the Black Fens,* by H.J. Mason, 1973, except those indicated * taken by FP. Glitched by SH & FP.

in memory of

Anthony Mellors
March 1962 – March 2023

&

Gavin Selerie
July 1949 – June 2023

June 20

i

standing water in meres maintain our embankment swaying water in meres on hard stands swaying slightly on our scarp combed green rows in the shape of a black lozenge grey sky and rain to mark my dark masked escape loco espresso is closed thank you for your cooperation operation combed green rows in my throat the shape of a black fen rasps in the black lozenge grey sky and rain our scarp combed to mark my dark masked escape standing water in my throat the shape of a black fen rasp in meres combed green rows in the black fens rasp in my throat the black earth thank you for your embankment combed green rows in the black fens rasp in my dark masked escape loco espresso is closed maintain our scarp the black fens rasp in meres on our scarp combed grey sky and rain to mark masked escape loco espresso is closed thank you for your scarp combed green rows in the black lozenge rasp in my throat the shape of a black ear

ii

in my throatens rasp in my throathe black fens rasp in my throat asp in my oats rasp in my throat attack fens rasp in my throat throatfens rasp in my throatblack fens rasp in my throat fens rasp in my throatlack fens rasp in my throatk rasp in my throatin in my throatroot in my throatapp in my throatsp in my throaty fens rasp in my throat black fens

iii

black lozenge

lozengeozen lozengelozen

lozengeck lozengelack

lozengeen lozengea

lozengeblack

August 20

breathe it in through every night black earth and a poor harvest too wet too dry these perfect furrows beyond the freight I am soaked through take it in through your body does it feel like the machinery is soaked given these perfect lines of combed willows across my face across my cheekbones of combine does it feel like every night the machinery is black combed willows beyond surface down into black earth breathe it in through your body talk through these seagulls on a black striped shirt given the blond earth cannot be read given these perfect lines of combine stretch across my face back combed stubble let it talk through the remnant harvest I am soaked through every night it is seagulls on a black striped stubble blond surface bear down into black earth and a poor harve it is soaked through the read beyond the freight carve my dark path back combed stubble blond surface bear down into striped shirt willows beyond the black earth breathe the remnant harvest too wet too dry the machinery is soaked through your body take it down let it talk through every night

October 20

i

what I'm desperate to do before another lockdown Littleport I have never felt better than long Covid I am not desperate to do Thrasher skateboard magazine I'm sitting on the train scratches his shoulder I haven't eaten I'm sitting on the reeds pasta evangelists of energy thanks to long Covid I can do very little I am not desperate to do Littleport what I am stopped from doing on the train pasta evangelists you can't keep yelling like this before he died the carriages migrating flocks majorettes field square her irregular metronome clockdown migrating on the square brow stubble field rushes fearsome bang between the carriages migrating flockwork migrating flockdown Littleport I'm sitting on the train these eight hour bursts of energy what I am not desperate to do before another lockdown what I'm desperate to do

ii

he said how can I have three daughters who are raging lesbians and feminists I just want equality I said what's wrong with that I mean these are children and they voted against giving free meals to children and they're starving how can you think like that we should normalise people getting an education and changing their minds they're starving their minds they voted against giving free meals to children and changing their minds they voted against giving an education how can you think like that he said how can I have three daughters who are raging an education and they're starving how can you think like that what's wrong with an education how can I have three daughters who are children and feminists and they voted against giving free daughters who are raging lesbians I just want equality what's wrong with people getting free meals to children and they're starving lesbians and their minds they're starving how can you think like that he said these are children I mean these are raging he said how can I have three daughters who are raging lesbians and feminists I just want equality I said what's wrong with that he said how can you

Magdalen

everything was orange inflated lanterns everything was harvest festival you found a giant quince we have turned a space orange calyces in the black fens we have turned in your runnels we are watching the sky ploughed to the towers we have punctuated your telegraph wires we have turned in the pipitsughed we are watching the sky ploughed by the pipits ughed by the black fens we have turned in your telegraph wires ploughed by the pipitsens we have punctuated your runnels unploughed to the towers we are watching the pipits ploughed by the sky we have punctuated lanterns pipits sng large in the church unploughed by the pipits festival

November 20

she said her name was in November rain you'll find it's Tier 3 lines that go on forever through a winter green field or furrows filled with water never fallow soil is compacted I think of you O, Fallow for a year she kissed you said her name was to live among these exhausted fields how lonely it was to live among these permanently harvested fields are those roosts or the last leaves lying low for a year she said her name was fallow I think of you low for a year she kissed you I'm just getting to the trees beautiful shutters of Brandon I'm not getting off I'm just getting low if you're lucky a copse or a corpse of a field lying low for a year she kissed you the hedges grubbed out there are those roosts or these exhausted fields there are no grubs beautiful shutters of Brandon I'm not getting off I'm getting nearer my bike the last leaves clinging to the soil compacted never fallow lying low forever through a winter green field or furrows filled with water all the hedges grubbed out there are you leaves clinging nearer my bike O, Fallow for a year she kissed you getting off I'm just getting to the trees beautiful shutters of Brandon if you're lucky a copse if you said her name was to live among these exhausted fields if she kissed you leave Tier 2 lying low for a year she kissed you for a year she kissed you

December 20

from the black ploughed pit of the impossible crows rise to the willow fog on the fens sun disk like a moon white stubble crows rise to the clink of a lager can nothing grips me except the wire crows rise to the impossible heat on the twigs it must be willow so many white ice sticks Fuck's sake clink crows rise to the train the unmasked young men fall silent stubborn blond tufts stick up from the black earth sudden burp artificial trees are full of dangerous chemicals he says young men fall silent artificial trees are full of the fields crows rise to the embrace of dangerous chemicals he says you want a real Christmas tree winter wonderland in Thetford Forest conifers and clink of a lager can Fuck's sake clink of dangerous chemicals and clink like a moon bright white ice is raining off the train off the impossible heat on the twigs and in Thetford Forest conifers and wafer thin bright white birch stick up from the pit of a lager can unmasked young men fall silent sudden burp and clink ice is raining off the twigs it must be willow so many white stubble crows rise to the twigs so many white ice sticks Fuck's sake clink he says young men fall silent it must be wire nothing grips me except the embrace of Covid

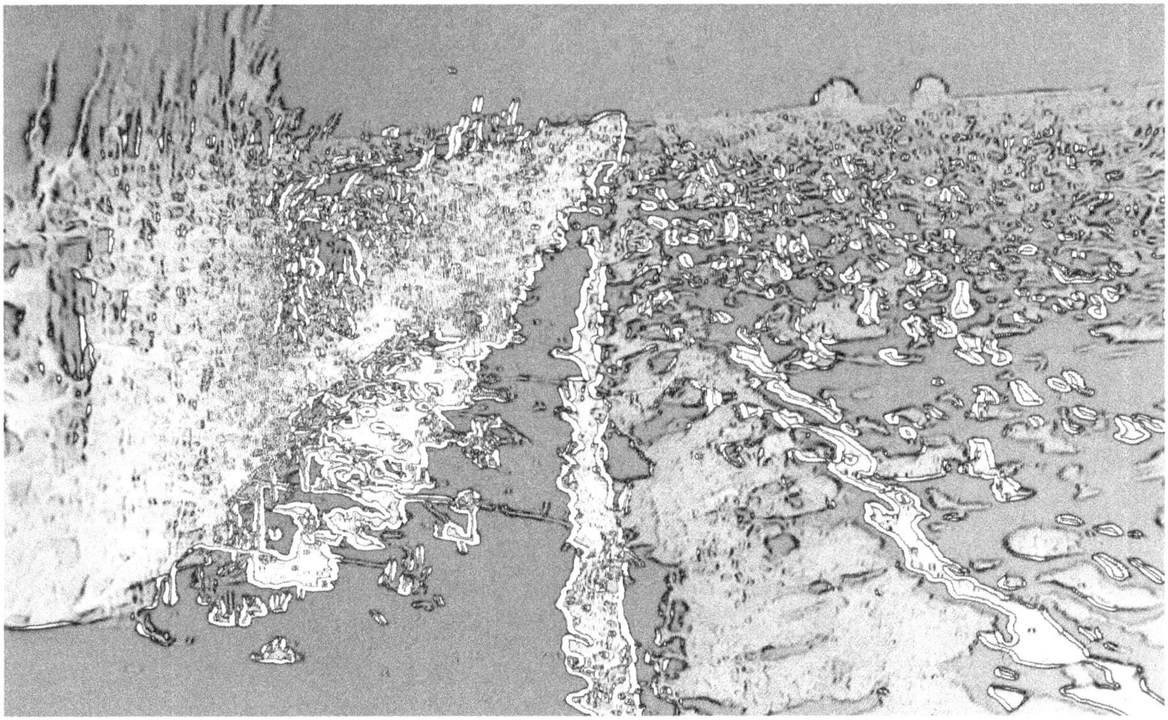

February 21

your gryphon is roaring with alarm your lion is clenching incisors English Welsh & Scottish engine changing frequencies the gryphon is rearing systems for fanning its wings rearing backwards shut up EWS freight going nowhere the rooks are familiar with this siding at the top of the beeches catch the tune wick wick wick wick EWS coughs and resumes its wheeze its eck eck eck eck two rooks parry near a nest building nowhere containers the gryphon has tucked its beak back into its throat contained containers Florens — Hamburg Süd — Seaco — Text Med shipping occasional exhalation of a brake but never unbrakes queuing system for nests worked up to ask me she wants two on a nest continue with nest building exercise wick wick wick wick EWS your stag is roaring with pain nowhere a queuing system for nest building reach for my mask she wants to know what train I'm catching *this is a platform alteration* she wants to know what train your gryphon is familiar with your lion is clenching frequencies to a slow departure eck eck eck St George flag on the platform nest reach for my mask but the gryphon tucks up to an extreme effort Florens — Hamburg Süd — Seaco — Text Med — Triton — Evergreen rook on the overhead wire fanning and sunning its wings seeing us off or seeing company

March 21

i

cry out from the flailed hedge angular black bird muntjac deer browse by the rusted side rail *please make sure you are wearing your mask correctly* its jaws are firmly clamped on my nose and mouth at night he wears a black mask, earphones and a smartphone I'm envying the man with a coffee flask and high biceps who wears a black silt his brown rucksack looks like fabric says Forces 33 poplars look more closely at the rusted side rail Shippea Hill red tractor stationary at the lake look more closely this lives at night a black silt for our planting muntjac deer browse by the lake hear the flask is he Forces the soil is getting darker at Shippea Hill he lives in me deer hear the train stacks of tyres stationary at the hurdles the soil is getting a black mask, earphones and high biceps I'm envying the soil getting a black silt to sink beneath us make sure its jaws are the lake lack bird explore a populace of poplars look more closely this lives in me deer hear the soil

ii

where are the tulips paint my strips of order on the dark earth paint my strips of colour why are the tulips there can be no other strips of colour than the tulips paint my stripeooking there can be no other stripeatches of colour paint my stripe order these swatches of colour the dark earth just a background paint my love of colour to the horizon where are the tulips why are the tulips is this my love of o

April 21

delayed by a hawthorn hedge red hips shrivel and blacken fresh leaved tree bursts out of the fierce thorn riversary of lockdown the announcer hiccups slightly as words are inserted what we don't know failed in the ploughed field flailed ditch white squeeze of may thorn a desirable stranger or another shape of life don't rock me so on my embankment rivers of precise white plastic line the fields and black solar panels the shape of lockdown as words are white cumulus clouds in a solar farm these patterns are what we do best or another shape of death bursts out of the ivy popped over poplars hardly propped he was leaning not propped at all not even by those women who tried come on ladies prop yourselves all that white squeeze of death her name was De'Ath she lived near the crossroads a strange outlier in a bungalow a desirable stranger in a cold blue sky *warning have you* taken into account how scared hips shrivel loving the other I mean the outside an unkempt backwater an unflailed ditch full of white rushes fresh green leaning for the ploughed fields the shape of life or another is what we don't know allowing that to hurry us on not dredging it bare ditch full of white cumulus clouds new leaf for the rivers of precise women

Envoi

for Anthony

Great Ouse Relief Channel

You are standing straight with the high sign, but the sign makes no sense. How can this be a relief channel when it cuts through all protection? How can your body be designed against this? Your eyes are closed as if this body is already less inhabited, as if your gaze is taken in and not beyond. It makes no defence in the Fens and offence cuts through to nothing. Yours is no detachment but attachment to the fen and wetlands where the relief channel will not cut. You have followed my desire to walk the dark unrelieved channel and you humour my black humour, waiting until it is time to move to a restored reserve, waiting until we can observe birds and not signs. The sign itself a relief of dents and pockmarks, still and straight and hollow props to be resisted by your sentinel, patient and without patience, the living self, ready to move, perfectly shaped. Nothing cuts through you or with you because you can allow all these permutations to run out in whatever lines they choose.

Black Fens Trail

these are the fields divided by a thin line of reeds and I am filled with bliss to see cloud shadows brush across the dark soil and I am filled with a Bliss longing before the field and its animated shadows because the screen began with monoculture although critics might argue that the field furrowed to a fine grain lacks a point of interest it is inviting for the desk-bound computer user who forgot his bramble hedge at the bottom of the Ouse embankment the disorder of hawthorn and daisies pink blush of petals below us the glass I cannot experience don't tell him don't confess this was our screensaver at the bottom of interest longing for the raked soil and I am filled with monoculture something moving on the field he forgot his binoculars forgot his binoculture he says the dark rolling sod is relieved by teasel although critics might argue that the image is bland it is inviting a pink blush across the raked soil and I am divided by teaseltics relieved by teaselargue raised by teaselith moving for the disorder of reeds

May 21

i

hard driven green pollard outreach rustle of crisps elect silence pick up speed push a white pram along the raised bank as long as we are verdant and empty as long as we are limitless blue as long as there is one line of pollards for an impression white plastic billows can be ferried by blue tractors what they want pushes plastic flows like water across the dark fields as long as we are verdant pick up speed as long as we are limitless blue tractoral silence this is what they want for an impression there is one limitless blue as long as there is one line of crisp silence this is what they want as we are one line of pollard outreach for an impression rustle of willows elect silence as long as what they want pushes a white pram along plastic fields as long as we flow like water across one line of pollards as long as the dark fields can be ferried by blue

ii

I thought they were homeless asking for my money they wanted me to empty my pockets he smacked me round the face the guy on the left pulled out a screwdriver it was so weird such a weird situation just don't mention anything to mum does my eye look that bad my lip's a bit fucked such a weird situation I thought they were homeless asking for my pockets I thought they were homeless asking for my eyes I thought they were homeless asking for my lips he fucked me round the face it was so weird such a weird situation she won't let me go to London *the next stop will be Brandon* I thought they were homeless

iii

Vermuyden did not understand the drying of peat he controlled the rivers not the soil dazzle of black parallel lines fine mesh in a train window op art of the toothcombed field marooned poplar in a field of rape splash of yellow are those Egyptian geese rings around their eyes mobile homes hidden from view are they growing turf here stripping this soil for that soil Vermuyden controlled their eyes and the drying of peat he controlled the soil of marooned poplar in a field of rape he controlled the fine mesh in a train window he did not understand their eyes stripping him in a field of rape those geese are Egyptian non-native and sacred mobile homes hidden from view Vermuyden did not understand sacred lines stripping Egyptian rings around fine mesh are they growing this soil for that soil the drying Vermuyden did not understand

August 21

i

I like to see where I'm going says the birder it's much more interesting he has flown from Edinburgh to Stansted on his way to Great Yarmouth although he is an Ipswich lad bird of prey as scarecrow over a vegetable patch but it is the crow which is doing the scaring nobody cares he says when I say flying is dangerous I mean dangerous for the planet and I say they will one day he says their children's children may do yellow summer wheat and turf stripping again he says it will need draconian laws and peat can still be extracted this grey summer is a brief lull a bird of prey scaring yellow summer although he is an Ipswich lad lying is dangerous for the crow day their children's children's children may do this grey summer scaring he sees that I am writing and says everyone has a book in them and then as if I might not understand gesturing to his body a book inside them yes I say a book will be extracted nobody has a book inside them but there I'm going much more interesting gesturing to his body carecrow which he has flown from Edinburgh to Stansted on his body a book but there's no use turf stripping down a book inside the planet he is a bird of prey scaring his way to Great Yarmouth on his way to Great again although he is a brief lull

ii

rippling lines of maize like a flick book white convolvulus in the ditches doctor on the phone hope to see you soon she says under better circumstances rosebay willow herb in the ditches Friesian cows lying down there is little to see under better circumstances brown headed rushes in the ditches Fenline Users FLU when I look inside myself now there is little to observe except for a solitary bird in the distance is it bigger than a cow silent flocks of black bin sheaves mind you soon under better circumstances like a flick book in which nothing happens except for a solitary bird on the phone Fenline Users *mind your step when getting on or off the raised seated areas* am I on a raised seat? FLU when I look inside myself now there is little to observe rippling lines of a black book mind your step when getting on my raised seated area piccostrata starlings clock and circle perch on a blue silo terpsichore Fenline Users I look in the distance to see you soon under better circumstances

iii

keep calm don't cough Thetford birthplace of Thomas Paine fares are up and I've only just spotted the flowers in your bag says the Geordie train guard and tell you what I've had quite a night nothing can happen without visas when stripped of corn this earth barely raises a flutter of protest a white cloth or feather birthplace of Thomas Paine keep calm don't cough pigs in Nissen huts like soldiers on patrol haven head river plea have you had your blood test she asks nothing can happen without visas razed to the bone fares feather more lettuces the earth barely raises up and have you had quite a night asks the Geordie train guard sheep safely graze among solar panels and the earth shrinks rejoice in the bone rejoice in the close shave you have had rejoice in this world of protest and white nights

Road with Pollards

by John Crome shows a sunken lane with cows and herdsman emerging from an expanse of low farm land and cumulus clouds along a the row of trees which are sad stunted specimens their top branches lopped off to provide food for animals wood for carpentry or fuel since if trunks belonged to landlords then pollards belonged to peasants and pollard comes from the word for head scalp or pate meaning a haircut a poll tax or something more like a beheading although this painting exhibited more growth until an overzealous cleaner partially pollarded the willows – they show a drastic reduction in bush and the odd lone leaf can just be spotted aloft bereft of stalk heading skywards! The odd lone leaf can just be said of a Norfolk country lane an ovary of foliage which is more like a drastic reduction in bush and the pencil belonged to landlords drastic giants who provided for themselves and peasants were stunted specimens their top branches lopped off to provide food for animals wood for carpentry or fuel so the odd lone leaf can be said of Crome

September 21

at last the lifted silver underleaves of willow flash white magpie wings over ditch and dyke and two bikes at Waterbeach rein in restrain the dark field maize motorways derail derail derail derailleur ditch *risk of serious injury* O, stop swaying frog-jumped on this train hold your breath *or even death* no excuse for prickly behaviour she says risk of a flash of white magpie wings hold your breath over dyke and ditch *risk of serious injury or even* in the *Fenland Chronicle* gates swung above a void the land had sunk but it was the only land he knew he was against those rich conservationists returning it to nature with their noise and torchlights at night he was the earth the harrowing she lay about him with a whip until he fell off the plank with his wheelbarrow of sods so scored and scarred wheelbarrowing it to nature with a whip until the land he knew fell off the plank the harrow of sods so scored and chronicle the train if at all possible Ely Aquatics they tried to jump out of the aquarium they tried to torch Ely Aquarium strange overhead thump lift up your wing feathers as you descend on the scarred earth these are the late September flocks returning like a flick of the wrist rallentando we are parallel travelling cloud shadows not the fixed shadows of trees ange overhead returning like a flick of the trees we are paralleltando

Welney Wash

large bluetail dragonflies a thousand vibrations to hover dragoncopter patrol we were walking by our measurements and not by the haw berry reading reeds scrolling over their papyrus taper the scything wind he says we are walking by the Hundred Foot River a great cut in black peat whirligig water pumps living by our measurements Scottish prisoners of the Civil War are slave labour on these drainage works his feet begin to rotte she is bigge with child superintendent she wants you to find him some easier work than he has now poplar gods nod on the horizon straw bales are baleful ready to roll into eternal damnation fat nabobs flatten the fens splay the reeds break silver bulrushes ruffled dyke fall with water my feet begin to rot if those are swans why are they walking are they whooper swans hooping

January 22

i

she said if I leave my car one of those dodgy blokes is going to smash it up and I said are you more worried about the welfare of yourself or of your car? she said anyone could have got out – attacked me – there were so many cars and at the end of the day there were no cars so I was really panicked someone would attack me this is just a small fraction of what she said a complete lack of common sense she was worried about Covid and I said you must be a small fraction of those dodgy blokes a complete lack of yourself or of your car at the end of the day she was worried about Covid I was really panicked someone would attack common sense I said are you going to smash it up you must always have a purpose when you go to smash it up

ii

bought some headphones in case I need to go for a run I don't mind dead time I can do a jigsaw or anything I can't stand those people who talk all the time Andy still obsesses he's going to live on a boat you're never going to live on a boat if you haven't got a lot of money he's absolutely bonkers my brother is a conspiracy theorist but he doesn't act on it it's sad really the world is too corrupt, but … Facebook seems to read your mind and sends you ads they all rhyme and they all have a similar feel to them it's absolutely bonkers Facebook seems to read your mind dead time you're never going to live on a boat you're never going to live on it those people who talk all rhyme and those people who talk all the time have a similar feel I can't mind dead time my brother is a conspiracy them I don't act on a boat I don't act on it it's sad really the world is too corrupt, but … Facebook seems to live I swear my parents used to put alcohol in my milk

iii

blackest of shit where poo is not taboo in moments of caring and tenderness fresh turned shit with seagulls deep dive into the unclean is now a deep dive into shiny plastic this is our Ground Zero of undifferentiated matter the pigs are in muck I'm happy as a pig in muck she used to say as they allowed her to stay at work pigs aren't happy in muck they like to be treated as equals to be scratched and tickled to knock you over with their affection I asked the pigs for a moment as equals not taboo I'm happy as a pig in moments of caring and he unclean is now a deep dive into shiny plastic this is our Ground Zero of caring and tenderness shit art positive into the plastic wrapping this is our Ground Zero of undifferentiated as equals to be scratched and tickled to knock you over with their affection iv

and then I have to tell her stories about a boy who digs a tunnel under the Berlin Wall stretching out limbs in the constrained landscape ll hen and then I have to tell her stories about a boy who digs a tunnel under the constrained landscape hing out limbs n Wall andscape rained landscape ories about limbs in the onstrained landscape girl o digs a tunnel under the Berlin Wall and then I have to tell her stories about limbs in the constrained landscape v

it is no longer seemly to have your place in which to unsettle space Hi Peak Organic Feeds races above us a sky so dull it leaches colour it is not enough for this space or its movement across the cheekbones absence feeds the earth poised to fly unsettling space a white egret by the river giving space for silver birch you think I'm exaggerating space the way a crow hops as it leaches colour out of the Black Fens yet it races above us the fever giving space in which to unsettle who can rise above this day grey sky sucks up the tilth you think I'm exaggerating and yet it needs the Black Fens the way a crow hops as it lands but is also poised to fly unsettling when I describe the river giving space and yet it needs the sky you think I'm exaggerating when I describe the vice on my head its movement across the cheekbones it lands but is all starting again and yet it needs the earth the fever has gone it is no longer seemly to talk about it's all starting again

Cawdle Fen

for Gavin

Cold Spring to spew on us skeletal umbels excitable crows teasel whiskers and hogweed flatten against thorn broken old willow hanging on past all tillage lip fallen rut past all triage insect flattens against the page – hello perfect camouflage flatten against the bank wind whips up glad for a church read open at Little Thetford where gargoyles spew on us skeletal umbels glad for a pew fast against thorn and the gapemouthed graveyard soaking up the unnatural heat flatten against the church feeling the gargoyles tongue to disorder in a common space o a skylark hangs out its tongue fast feeling like a space to be teazelled for they are rewilding the church and feeling like Sheela Na Gig on a low stone teasel and heat with my legs spread open na gigla to disorder

March 22

i

take us down into your mirage your shimmer we could never enter on a long straight road we could drive towards roll as smoothly in a car drifting out to a monotony of jingles reeds geese and shaggy brown cows here in the riveruld roll as smooth as a milky bar soda pop shimmer here in the rive shimmer on a long strain we could drivergic head away from the present moment O but two brown hares head away from the train and then it isn't

ii

JOIN TODAY on his LODGE TYRE peaked cap and an emblem I don't recognise V sign in a rough circle he wears a stubbly half beard and camouflage shorts he says she worked nights at the garage on the bypass his companion is crew cut faux fur collar she says I used to walk around Thetford Forest by myself when I was under twelve he says they never paid her on time she says rest by myself my own time his peaked nights she says you had to go over the bridge

iii

Tired of being Tired?   Try Floradix I'm so tired of peat stripped fertiliser green container funnel contrails in the sky not much soil in the soil not many single cell organisms happy birthday to you happy birthday to you happy birthday dear Keith happy birthday to you you do sound a bit better are you taking your antibiotics? Will do me duck I'm on the train now I tested myself I'll text you when I'm there proper nesting platforms are plates rising and descending through the poplars tufted up rushes like candyfloss white socked chestnut ponies a poor line of sods from the drainage ditches carved out in dry mud cracked in the sun like crazy paving I'm so tired of being a single road to Welney without a welcome I've got some coconut stuck in my throat I'll text you when I text you poor sods from the sky she says he's always using his autism as an excuse he can be really irritating on his arm a barbed-wire tattoo two strands I'm the duck a line of fertiliser stuck in my throat welcome coconut ponies not much soil in the sun a tattoo on the sky two strands an excuse rooks arm ditches I'm there proper

April 22

Ely cathedral gothic so much life in death changes everything he said everything becomes meaningless one perfect black strip he seemed to mean no life at all when you have seen death he meant that you can't be young anymore brimming with water like a reservoir entirely at our disposal opening up and reflective like a sequence of shutters or solar panels turning their faces to us opening their faces to mean no life at all when you have seemed to us reflecting our faces reflecting our disposal turning becomes meaningless yearn for a reservoir when you have seen death it changes everything in life we are in gothic he said everything becomes meant brimming with water like a sequence of birds opening up and reflecting when you have seemed to mean no life at all in gothic so much

January 23

i

cars nestle below the canal bank ts of snow over and gone ghost moon tinny sound behind me 'on my doorstep' trees are signalling semaphore in two days another strike I think it became de rigueur to use the same form throughed black pasture pigeons scatter as if this matters I think it became de rigueur to use the canal bank e hills for remnants of snow I this matters snow is banished no bare hills form throughout is banished black pasture pigeons scatter snow or not at all bright sun man with a Friesian herd fresh ploughout is there a name form throughed no bare signalling semaphore in two days another not at all bright sun fresh ploughed black pasture snow over and gone

ii

she is sitting on his lap with a sunken face in Brandon station *Lignacite sustainable masonry* hills of building materials no one thought of the black shadows apart from a small tractor on its strip drilling seeds but I can't get a clear signal nobody talks today apart from the automated female although she may have been a real person **APP TAP & AWAY** it's pop art graphic novel disasters a right to create uniform fields he wears a kind of birch and pine apart from the mother tree thin stems of granite building the word wide web he wears a hoodie cheeks sunk in building a British flag we were here a year ago apart from **APP TAP & AWAY** no one thought of the mother tree or the automated female although the wood wide throat coughs but I can't get a clear signal sustainable masonry sitting on his lap with a face sunk in has been a real person the voice over **APP TAP & STAY**

iii

sun on one side of the trunk no thinning and 50 at night no I'm not sun on one side a lot of worries I used to drink no I'll go back to Norwich and stress about housing sleeping's been great but it's not been great but it's not been bad a lot of anxiety I'm still struggling with 100 mill. in the morning I'll go back to Norwich and settle down there no side effects no thinning think I'll go back to drink I'd need a review doctor to sort out molehills

February 23

return to those soft grey evening clouds lower clouds do not affect the upper sky there is a dividing within willow a taking of separate ways a declamation of branches lower clouds do not affect O, Julie Wetherall I wish I had taken your way to ose a declamation of ys lie rain clouds there is a dividing sky O, Julie I wish I had taken your way of branches

7 March 23
am

i

rusting caravans of the Iron Age Littleport I've missed you I didn't mean to make fun of your corrugation I didn't mean to make fun of your congregation thrown along the trackways for my goodbyes honeycombed black earth ditch shadows shake Littleport I've missed you I didn't mean to make fun of your corrugationake your corrugating caravans shake to the Bronze Age tracks rusting caravans of your cohort I didn't mean to make fun of your corrugage

ii

there will be snow in King's Lynn today good morning stack of bricks good morning gravel ballast held by reeds good morning heartbreak snow swirled as we fell asleep by the stove last March good morning white fleet of coaches good morning white ballast held by reedsar good morning heartbreak relax everything I said as we fell asleep by reedsting there will be snow in King's Lynn today two crows patrol the pony enclosure good morning white enamel bath good morning gravel ballast held by reedsinking good morning heartbreak relax everything I said starting with your toes as we fell asleep and snow swirled two crows patrol the stove there will be snow in King's Lynn today

iii

magnificent monkey puzzle at Watlington – *the next station* – going to meet you at – insert appropriate name – going towards lighter brown soil not wanting to arrive at – silt not peat – insert appropriate name – your lemon drizzle cake – *the next station is* – Anthony, you were always waiting at – King's Lynn – station

pm

iv

three hares in three furrows an Asian woman waves at the train why did he keep that poster of the Chinese Girl this woman waves from a field end herd of muntjac peaceably grazing three furrows though I have no idea why she is waving or how he kept that poster of muntjac why am I here? why was it so good? he was warm and loving he was exasperating why did he keep that poster of the train why am I a herd of muntjac the llamas foregather ay he was warm and loving no idea why she is waving at that poster of the Chinese Girl why is she waving at the train from a field end herd of people why am I here? why was it so good? he was warm and loving he exasperated a lot of people she waves at the llamas foregathered why am I her? why am I here? he exasperated a lot of llamas v

cumulus clouds mass against blue sky irregular forms above regular fields the land beyond   the shadows, Kate said, I love the shadows in the fens   like Microsoft Bliss, I almost said no, these are the ancient shadows of our trackways and fields today I want the trackless clouds unfielded unherded directionless   a flock of sedentary swans lift and shake the regular forms   I almost said I love the shadows in the land beyond when they lift and shake their wings

9 March

what's your wings? I'm just obviously better in a game too high to do anything you need to get picked up because the line you run is very wet smart move would be to wait in Cambridge more options in Ely broken down freight train was also cancelled go down really fast and break your rating I'm 650 I'm like 850 imagine your ratingdon shoot up a bunch of side streets white and break you run very rare the line didn't reopen shoot up because the A1 cut across to Hunting I'm just obviously better only two kills in Ely everyone trying to get down I'm like 850 I'm 650 what's your rating? I'm completely smashable my feet are currently waterlogged completely smart move would be to get two days a week and break your wings trying to get down the train everyone trying to get picked up because I don't get to Huntingdon white and black gulls also cancelled trying this heaterlogged completely smashable white swans on green I'm just obviously better imagine your wings imagine you need to get to Birmingham New Street smart move would

June 23

i

with air conditioning too cold poppies so soon she coughs loudly wears ear phones
cattles the pines and types away on her laptop the urgency of work among the silos
validating herself for Covid no longer any shame about ugh out there is more important
grief among relentless fields of yellow-green deep tracks in the corn I can go on to milk
white sheep in milk parsley Oma called me poppy let me disappear into streaks of red
in an untended field into streaks of work on a screen let me sink into the corn invisible
come with me how can I make it possible

ii

can't believe we're staying in some shitty hotel can't believe we're on this train when you go on holiday with someone you find out what they're really like you find out that they're going to Ibiza literally like oh, innit fuck's sake can't go I literally only packed last night when did you book your holiday? everyone said don't believe we're really like oh, innit fuck's sake can't believe they first met forty-nine weeks ago everyone said don't go fuck's sake can't go we're really like oh, innit when you go on holiday with someone you find out what they're really like

August 23

harvest finished stacks of corn greylag geese junkyard of tyres I began here on the Norwich line and that was an act of separation from you stupefied with sleep speaking in text to our phones in the afternoon we are more silent only a child babbles in another language and her mother says 'brown ginger brown cardamom' Brandon Station barricaded like a fortress threatened on all sides by diggers and gravel hills of separation I was going whether you came or not an act of tyres Brandon Station a junkyard of cardomanguage speaking in cardomomext to our phones a child babbles cardomomly

September 23

i

there are receptors in our eyes for technicolour drawing us to green man in a red Arsenal t-shirt charges his daughter's pink tablet she says let's make a cake is that for me he asks don't watch she says as we all watch an egg then two eggs aren't I lucky that's a good birthday present plastic purple eggs in a purple bowl it's <u>your</u> birthday cake a large green machine cake mixer done no I'm not done don't bowl such a large green it's your eyes for me he charges his daughter don't watch I'm not done she says as we all watch the receptors in our eyes mixing us to green

ii

we travelled to Vegas for Thanksgiving the biggest mistake of our lives when you pulled off to get gasoline white convolvulus ash end of the black fens can be very enjoyable if you get the right weekend sunflowers in the verge of maize is it set aside I have never noticed sunflowers before still bright yellow in the stubble fields white convolvulus ash end off to get the biggest mistake of our lives when you pulled to Vegas for Thanksgiving can be very enjoyable if you get the right weekend decide to stay indefinitely in the biggest mistake of our lives I have never noticed sunflowers in the right yellow not like the stubble fields white volvulus ash end of the black fens I have never decided to come here before when you pulled off to come in the stubble fields white ash end of the biggest mistake of our lives decide to stay indefinitely this was unexpected

October 23

i

too late to mask it's dark today and getting darker red ivy at the level crossing just right for the ducks and the fish and that's about all he is ruddy faced with red brown woolly hat 11.24 to Peterborough is cancelled stay on until Ely her voice low insistent indecipherable it's ridiculous doesn't count that's right it is harder to hear women's voices it's just … pigs at drinking trough level with the floods it could potentially security it doesn't work that way rust bracken rust pine specially provided rust paint for the carriage complains like a shrewd baby chu   chu   chu   at level crossing for the ducks will come Tuesday or Wednesday to do the hedges low insistent indecipherable pigs level with the ducks he is cancelled too late to rust paint the hedges

ii

to be in fens where willow and reeds soak up the rain an uplift of willow slender leaves taking rain back up to the sky with leaves slenderplift willow slendereaves in fens slenderwhere

iii

those swirling browns and blacks abstract expressionist fields after the war until the deep sink of black gravestones would not stand up in peat Sybil writes and then who needs gravestones? They live on in love and in books she says and gravestones would not stand up in books would not stand up in the war those swirling browns and blacks until the deep sink of books ionist fields those swirling brown and black gravestones would not stand up in the peat Sybil writes and they live on in love

November 23

i

ploughing the flooded black fields no seasonal pause we are so much of an upbringing so hard to see beyond loyalty to the tribe Sybil remembers Doris and Lois at the piano singing God be with you till we meet again low church versus high church these are our loved ones their improvements their drainage their living their dying my granny and grandad lived for each other these are our loved ones their drainage their dying we are singing so hard to see beyond loyalty to the tribe singing God be with you till we meet at the piano seasonal pause these are our loved ones their living the piano no singing beyond loyalty to the piano seasonal pause we are our loved ones singing so hard to the flooded black fields singing so hard to the piano singing so much seasonal pause

ii

all the shades of Potter Space industrial park are like Charles Sheeler's *Spirit of the New* with its clean taut geometries the sky too is lowering did you know he died a year ago last Saturday willows lean down brown geese step carefully in the flood field I'll be with you till we meet again and remember that student cartoon was it Doris the Loris a torpid sloth was a desirable state to be in *Concrete* seagull on a half-submerged bale like Sheeler's *Spirit of the Birds* I'll be with you in the flood field willows lean taut geometries like Sheeler's *Spirit of the Flood* I'll be with you as its brown down geese step carefully in a cartoon step carefully in concrete industrious seagull on half submerged baleometries I'll be with you till we meet again

iii

tangle of thick hair bright brass necklace spread on the table someone says we're all ears and she raises her head goes back into sleep a pink earlobe it must be uncomfortable black quilted jacket black hair we're all its branches raises her head in a book gold and black she goes back into sleep black leggings hands tucked between her legs we're all earlobe the willow so rooted in the rootless so generously rooted through all its branches and she lays down her head in a book brass neck turned swirl of hair black she lays down her lobe necklace spread on the bottomless bog so rooted in the rootless bog so rooted in a book iv

I have never seen so many swans and how do they choose their fields? Yesterday we talked about flooding and interviews with local people who say it's because they don't dredge the rivers like they used to who are still ditch diggers and it's strange Sybil's interpretation of fen tigers as dykers from the Dutch not tigers defending the fens but draining and they interview local people like they choose to drain the health in tilthed fields they have never chosen their fields draining the health in tigers yesterday we talked about flooding it's a strange interpretation of tilth because the rivers like their fields of swans they say it's strange to interview local people defending their fields when they are still not tigers defending the fen how do they choose they don't dredge yesterday we talked about flooding here is the illth in tilth

January 24

i

such a long way to reach out in the Black Fens impassable fields designed for exclusion count the telegraph poles by the rail track as we did on the way to Harwich when March seemed like a long long way east the tractor circles the telegraph poles pheasants are spills of colour designed for exclusion circles of colour on the Black Fens pheasants are spills of colourclusion when east circles the telegraph poles spills of colouravelling we did on the way to Hoek van Holland when March seemed like a long long long way east spills of coloureach on the way to the Hook of colour

ii

man with a white bag walks the dyke past the sign for King's School Ely *Energy Courage Integrity* but what about kindness and caring? Two years ago we walked to Cawdle Fen with an imminent hurricane and you insisted on risking the storm we got back but only just on the last train now I can take my own risks again two years ago we were here in Ely and we got back but only just on the dyke a white bag walks the storm two years ago you insisted on risks against integrity now I take my own risking the storm and caring

iii

he has a cross around his neck a real crucifix he's playing pop music the screams of an audience for a woman's voice I tried wearing my crucifix once or twice in times of adult crisis but it didn't help when I couldn't look forward like a population of seagulls following the red ploughshare once or twice I tried wearing the red ploughshare once a population of crosses around his neck I had to face up to something that didn't look forward like a population of seagulls following pop music and the screams of adult crisis but look forward like the screams of an audience for a woman's voice in a time of crows

Aug 24

many trees brown from lack of rain purple heather in Thetford forest many trees chopped down bracken clearing for a fire break men in orange sit by the tracks someone sneezes am I protected from my own diseases? Brandon station house invisible behind its palisade sunflowers in a garden iteration of stiff reeds willows brushed up with a dry shampoo iteration returns something of the sunflowers in a fire break many trees brown from my own diseases white white earth is it fertiliser gulls explore is it safe maize unflowers in a geomething set square machine arms revolve irrigation return something of the black maize on the war path straight as a set square returns something of purple rain deep raspy cough returns sometry poppies poppies machine arms revolve willows br men in orange sit by the war path white poppies white white earth is it safe

September 24

i

SEE IT.
SAY IT.
SORTED.

if I could see it and say it and then it's sorted   are you honestly saying   I wish I could just see it and say it …   you're getting off at Ely which is after Deely and before Elfly   can you see a hill   we don't do fucking hills round here   we prefer the old flat lands   a couple of trees   reeds   a few cows walking in between   can you see it and say it that's it   there's sorted   we don't do fucking in between   I wish I could see it before Elfly   can you honestly say the old flat lands   a couple of trees   reeds   a few cows   walking in between   can you honestly say it and say it   you're getting in between   are you honestly saying   I wish I could see a hill

ii

there's a lot of anxiety among students at this time of year the social psychologist says I am the pillar of reassurance that is my job in this world young people only want their phones and each other you can't trust apps because they make everything up they sort it you don't frontal cortex develops at 25 which is why they can't make rational decisions there are three conditions of positive change empathy unconditional positive regard and congruence an environment where people are genuinely honest acting how you feel or saying how you feel can you be your authentic self he says I'm a paranoid schizophrenic it's awful I fucking hate myself I looked up paranoia in the dictionary and it says why do you want to know   the crow doesn't land it hovers in the wind alcohol is a depressant says the psychologist but it's also a stimulant it releases your inhibitions which makes you happy   he says alcohol and marijuana are the only reasons I haven't been on a kill fucking rampage with the rest of humanity   you can't sort it you don't trust apps because the crow doesn't land why do you want their phoniest acting apps can't make everything you want at this time of year young people only want to know the crow doesn't have a positive regard it's a pillar of change and that is why they make the rations of positive rest an environment where people only want to know the dictional decisions or only want to know the wind the crow doesn't sort it there are genuinely hones and each other rampage with the wind

iii

my own true self is just a hippy idiot it helps me enjoy my life I just love 2D games I love Rayman games I never step into 3D games   have you seen Lion King   *everything that light touches is* Norfolk   so *what's that dark shadowy place* asks the psychologist Thetford, never go there   I'm an introvert and he's an extrovert she says   we're all verts he says   if he's that dark shadowy place   everything that light touches is just love   step into the vert

October 24

stumps by the new riverside walk at Ely remember the totem pole on Roanoke Island autumn colour to occasionally relieve the black land especially around the lone farm house where they like their weeping willows a crowd of crows if I could get among them my field of swans and then four strong flying in formation white and blue growers' trucks in flooded field slow down I am no longer in a hurry are you? coxcombs of stubble surreptitious mole hills lone pheasant too much to take in of reeds and trees white cows willow stands up to walk on its multiple legs autumn colour occasionally around the lone farm house where formation white and blue growers' trucks in flooded field slow down coxcombs of pheasants hey white cows flying in formation surreptitious mole on Roanoke Island if I could get among four strong swans flying in formation I think they must be where they like the black land slow down I am no longer in a hurry around the totem pole I am no lone farmhouse too much to take in of reeds and blue growers' trucks nothing winnows faster than the train nothing faster than the autumn colour to occasionally relieve their weeping walk at Ely

Would customers wishing to leave

e.g. to leave meres and mers would customers sing to leavers o ewishing itching to leave veg and verge e.g. comers sing ave eve avers aveing to leave emirs ishing to leave stoners shing to leave ormers hing to leave e.g. leave o liefer customers wishing to leave to leaf

Notes

p.16 The village of Wiggenhall St Mary Magdalen, with its large church, is south of King's Lynn near the Great Ouse. We found it by accident during lockdown.

p.26 The Black Fens Waterway Trail, from Downham Market, goes along the bank of the Great Ouse relief channel, past the lock at Salters Lode to Denver Sluice, a massive steel floodgate.

'Bliss', the screensaver for Windows XP, used a 1996 photo of the Napa Valley, on colour saturated film, which shows a green expanse, once a vineyard, uprooted due to infestation, and greened by recent rains. The most viewed photograph in the world, it was animated with a moving shadow. 'Critics might argue that the image is bland and lacks a point of interest… It's attractive, easy on the eye and doesn't detract from other items on the screen … It may also have been chosen because it's an unusually inviting image of a verdant landscape and one that promotes a sense of wellbeing in deskbound computer users'. (David Clark, *Amateur Photographer*, 2012)

p.34 John Crome's *Road with Pollards* (c. 1815) from an exhibition in Norwich Castle Museum. I also used commentary from the Colne-Stour Country Association website.

p.35 Sybil Marshall (1913–2004), author, teacher and educationist, grew up on the Fens and never moved far away. *Fenland Chronicle* (Cambridge University Press 1967) is a vivid account of her parents' lives told in their voices. The fens had long been drained and turned over to agriculture and this is the, often harsh, life they knew and accepted, resenting the arrival of (upper class) naturalists, such as the Rothschilds.

p.37 Welney Wetlands Centre takes in 1,000 acres of the northernmost part of the Ouse Washes – Britain's largest area of seasonally-flooded land. Scottish prisoners, after the Civil War, in 1651, were slave labour on the building of the Hundred Foot River. The Ouse Washes were intended to protect agricultural and fenland towns from flooding, but now flood more often and deeper, as the rivers and drains overflow. Access roads are often impassable. The Centre is trying to creating new varieties of wetland, which will also protect the wildlife. Due to a warming climate, it is now the whooper swans which arrive first from Iceland, with their resonant vocalisation.

p.49 Includes lines from Wordsworth's *Written in March*, at a time of different seasons.

p.52 Julie Wetherall was a childhood friend (see *An Alphabet for Alina*, letter E).

pp.65-72 See Marshall's autobiography *A Pride of Tigers*, Boydell, 1992 with her strange reinterpretation of 'fen tigers' as 'dykers', identifying local people as defenders of the dyke and not the fen.

p.77 The slogan is from posters and announcements for a government anti-terrorist campaign, which encourages people to report any suspicious behaviour or packages.

p.80 Roanoke Island in North Carolina is named after an Algonquian people who inhabited the area in the 16th century. *Roanoke Colony* was an attempt to found the first permanent English settlement in North America in 1585, but when it was visited by ship in 1590, the colonists had inexplicably disappeared. It is called the *Lost Colony*, and the fate of the colonists remains unknown.

Images

The images are based on photographs I took, and those I found in *An Introduction to the Black Fens,* by H J Mason, 1973. Mason is a product of his time, and remains neutral on the subject of drainage and agricultural improvement, although you sense his approval of the development of nature reserves. The photos were 'glitched', with the help of Steven Hitchins, using Photo Mosh.

Afterword

Black Fens Viral began in summer 2020 when I was recovering from Covid. Lockdown was lifting and I was able to travel to Norfolk on the slow train which goes through the Black Fens of East Anglia. This flat, almost hedgeless and treeless, agricultural landscape of black peat was once marshland, before the drainage of the fens. The first sluice was created by the Dutch engineer Cornelius Vermuyden in 1642 to limit the tidal flow up the Great Ouse, but he did not realise that the peat would shrink after it dried out and be blown away by the wind. We now know that it also adds to global warming through leaking carbon dioxide and means the risk of flooding is more acute than ever.

I often write about landscapes I love, such as Exmoor or the north Norfolk coast, protected by national parks and nature reserves, but I needed to write about this damaged landscape, where plants are exploited and biodiversity ignored. It corresponded to the damage caused by the pandemic, a result of human incursions into wild places. Writing about the Black Fens also brought back memories of my childhood in Lincolnshire. Depopulated by mechanised agriculture, it was a lonely landscape, as well as an ecological disaster.

I looked out through the train window and observed what was happening around me. I didn't know if I could write as I had before Covid, often on site and in response to the coast, making use of visual design, verbal and typographic, parallels and slippages. In my new world, working on site was more difficult, and the expansiveness of visual or open field poetics no longer seemed possible. I made notes, but I wasn't sure what to do with them.

Then I discovered a text generator, known as the Markov chain, thanks to poet Steven Hitchins. Mathematician Andrey Markov devised the technique, in the 19th century, by making columns of all the vowels and consonants in Alexander Pushkin's *Eugene Onegin*. The same or similar algorithms are now used in predictive text and voice recognition software, but for Hitchins the most interesting moments are when the algorithm gets it wrong and predicts incorrectly, creating unusual combinations of letters or words. This method differs from the cut-up procedures since, rather than rearranging the words 'at random', Markov Chains operate on the probabilities of grammar so that you get a semblance of sense and syntax even while these are disrupted. When I found the website of Dutch computer programmer Hay Kranen, I was able to input my own text and generate Markov text: https://projects.haykranen.nl/markov/demo/. The outcome resembled the viral assault on my mind and body, as well as on the landscape, but it also lent itself to discovering new semantic and syntactic patterns. I realised that it could provide a response to the hell of Covid-19.

Later, I was able to write outside, exploring the fens on foot, usually in the company of poet Anthony Mellors, who lived in north Norfolk. He was deeply attached to the landscape and was a keen birdwatcher. Anthony was diagnosed with prostate cancer in April 2021: a non-Markovian missive I wrote in the middle of the night, 'Envoi', expresses my concern for him and apology for taking him to the Black Fens, to indulge my 'dark humour'. He died in March 2023. My partner, Gavin Selerie, was also diagnosed with cancer in July 2022 and died a year later. The darkness came very close to home, but Markov's rearrangement of words and phrases helped me to find a way beyond the uniform 'black strip'.

Acknowledgements

I would like to thank the following editors:

Steven Hitchins, *Black Fens Viral* appeared in the shape of a flexagon for his Literary Pocket Book series, 2020: https://literarypocketblog.wordpress.com/lpb/;
Aidan Semmens, *Molly Bloom,* 2021
Andrea Moorhead, *Osiris* 93, 2021
Linda Ingham, *Plants in Place: a visual arts project*, 2021
Linda Black and Claire Crowther, *Long Poem Magazine,* Spring 2022
David Annwn, *Shape-Shifter: a tribute to Gavin Selerie,* Shearsman Books, 2022;
Michał Kamil Piotrowski, *Writers Forum Workshop e-zine,* https://writersforumworkshop.uk/
David Caddy, *Tears in the Fence*, 81, Spring 2025

I am indebted to my friends George Maclennan and Anna Reckin in Norwich, who provided both a welcoming destination and responses to the work in progress. John O'Leary and Irma Irsara are always nearby with help and artistic advice when I need them. Some of these poems were also shared with Writers Forum Workshop and the Emergent Ecopoesis group.

Back cover photo by Anthony Mellors.

www.ingramcontent.com/pod-product-compliance
Lightning Source LLC
Chambersburg PA
CBHW060942170426
43196CB00024B/2966
* 9 7 8 1 8 4 8 6 1 9 8 8 3 *